Lamar Jackson: The Inspiring Story of One of Football's Star Quarterbacks

An Unauthorized Biography

By: Clayton Geoffreys

Visit my website at www.claytongeoffreys.com
Cover photo by All-Pro Reels is licensed under CC BY-SA 2.0 / modified from original

Table of Contents

Foreword

Lamar Jackson has only played professional football for a little more than two years at the time of this writing. Yet, he has already accomplished so much in that time. Jackson has been named the NFL Most Valuable Player (being the second player to do so on a unanimous selection) and has set records for the most rushing yards in a season by a quarterback. We should not be surprised; since his college days, Jackson has been an electrifying offensive force to be reckoned with. At Louisville, Jackson won a Heisman along with a number of other college accolades. Hopefully we'll see much more of Lamar Jackson's ascent to the upper echelon of quarterback greats for years to come. Thank you for purchasing *Lamar Jackson: The Inspiring Story of One of Football's Star Quarterbacks*. In this unauthorized biography, we will learn Lamar Jackson's incredible life story and impact on the game of football. Hope you enjoy and if you do, please do not forget to leave a review!

Also, check out my website at claytongeoffreys.com to join my exclusive list where I let you know about my latest books. To thank you for your purchase, you can go to my site to download a free copy of *33 Life Lessons: Success Principles, Career Advice & Habits of Successful People*. In the book, you'll learn from some of the greatest thought leaders of different industries on what it takes to become successful and how to live a great life.

Cheers,

Clayton Geoffreys

Visit me at www.claytongeoffreys.com

Introduction

When we gather around and discuss the most exciting players in the NFL today, typical names that come to mind include Patrick Mahomes, Kyler Murray, Derrick Henry, Tom Brady, and Christian McCaffrey.

However, over the last year, a new name has emerged and potentially topped that list: Lamar Jackson. The Baltimore Ravens star quarterback has taken the NFL by storm with his ability to make remarkable and mind-blowing plays with both his arm and his legs and has already broken dozens of NFL records with more certainly to follow.

There have been successful running quarterbacks in the NFL before. Roger Staubach is probably one of the first names that come to mind for many old school fans for his scrambling ability. But in terms of ethnicity, it was Randall Cunningham who really paved the way for black quarterbacks to excel in the league with how he was able to generate plays with his arm and feet.

Since then, guys like Steve McNair, Michael Vick, Cam Newton, Warren Moon, Donovan McNabb, and Russell Wilson have come along, making the black quarterback a weapon and asset in the league.

The unfortunate and, at times, racist, criticism aimed at a lot of black quarterbacks in past eras has been that "their accuracy does not match their running ability." Doug Williams and Warren Moon were accurate passers but were not as big a running threat as Cunningham. Vick's speed transcended the game to a new level, but his accuracy was his biggest detriment. Old stereotypes and racial barriers have been broken and transcended as mindsets evolve. Today, guys like Wilson and Murray are becoming MVP-like quarterbacks with how they can run and throw accurately. And now along comes Lamar Jackson, who is performing at such a remarkable level and at such a young age that he may very well someday eclipse them all.

Jackson is unique in that he is a running back with tremendous speed while lining up as a quarterback and making plays with his arm. If there is anyone who questions his ability, look no further than his 2019 season where he won the NFL's Most Valuable Player Award. That season, Jackson broke the all-time record for most rushing yards by a quarterback gaining 1,209 yards on the ground. Not to be forgotten, Jackson also threw for 3,127 yards, finishing first in total touchdowns and touchdown percentage, first in quarterback rating, third in overall rating, ninth for completion percentage, and 10th in interception percentage. These statistics prove Jackson did not just get it done with his legs, he also got it done with his arm.

Jackson's 2019 season was beyond comprehension. He led the Ravens to the best record in the NFL, 14-2, and already has them succeeding in 2020 with one of the AFC's top records. Unfortunately, the 2019 season came to an end with an upset loss to the Tennessee

Titans, but it had much more ups than downs when Jackson reflected on his record-breaking season. Through his first 31 starts in the league, Jackson became the first player in NFL history to surpass 3,000-plus passing yards and 1,500-plus rushing yards in his first two seasons in the NFL.

In 2019, Jackson also set the all-time Ravens franchise passing record (which includes the team's history in Cleveland when they were the Browns). His 36 touchdowns were more than Vinny Testaverde's 33 with the team when they were the Browns in 1996.

It would be a dishonor to great legends and current stars like Randall Cunningham and Russell Wilson to say Jackson has transformed the position. As already mentioned, the running quarterback has been around for some time, and Michael Vick is probably the most comparable to Jackson because of his incredible quickness. But Jackson has taken it to a new level. Jackson ran the ball 176 times in 2019, an NFL record, and was only topped by 22 running backs for most rushing attempts.

What is most amazing, though, is that Jackson is not entirely happy with his image as a running quarterback. "I hate running," Jackson said. "I only do it when I have to, but my job is to get the ball to the receivers, the tight ends, the running backs."

He wants to be a passer first, and if he were to never run again and just be a pocket passer, he would still be one of the best quarterbacks in the league. He has the accuracy, the poise, and the arm to succeed at the highest levels.

Young adults everywhere have begun to look up to Jackson for many different reasons, not just because of his playing ability, but also for his character and positive attitude. He is different than a lot of athletes you see on television. Those who know Jackson describe him as playful and funny and "very real," which is encouraging given that the world today is filled with a lot of "fake" athletes who present a certain public persona but may be very different in private. Jackson's teammates also describe him as dedicated and hard-working. He hates to lose and is a leader both on and off the field. They say he continues to mature and improve because he is driven to get better and does not accept failure.

"What makes him special is his personality and easygoingness," Nick Boyle said. "When a play goes wrong or right, you look at him because he is the leader of the offense and he has a smile on his face and ready to move onto the next play. He is not going to yell at everyone, he holds himself accountable. He has this happy calmness that he brings to the team. When things don't go well, he's still OK."

Teammates love players like Jackson. The game of football is stressful on a multitude of levels and Jackson helps make it fun for others while pushing them hard at the same time. He is easy-going, yet competitive. He is fun, yet determined. He is always smiling and happy, yet on the field, he will run you over and make you pay if you make a mistake. He is a unique breed in the league and is looked up to by millions of young football fans all around the country.

What makes Lamar Jackson's story so inspirational is how he fought through adversity early in life to get to where he is today. Jackson grew up in poverty with his parents and lived in a financially challenged area of Florida near Pompano Beach. His father and grandmother played big roles in bringing him up very early on, but then one day he tragically lost them both in the same day, an event which traumatized him and his family when he was just eight years old.

He persevered because of two things: family and football. The family leaned on each other during those difficult days and his mother became the perfect role model for him. She pushed him to excel in football, a sport that his father had begun coaching him in when he was just a little boy. She became his number one coach. Jackson was talented as a quarterback, throwing the ball further than a lot of high school kids could at the age of just 10. He idolized Michael Vick growing up and wanted to be a quarterback just like him, making electrifying plays with his legs while also being able to chuck the ball more than 50 yards down the field.

As one would imagine, Jackson was fast as a child and excelled as a track athlete along with football. He won Player of the Year honors in high school both as a football player and as an overall athlete. He attended The University of Louisville and continued to advance his game, winning multiple awards there, including the Heisman Trophy. He helped produce winning seasons at Louisville, even getting them into the top-five in the country.

Many did not think his style of football would work in the NFL, however. They felt he was too much like

Robert Griffith III, who was a similar college athlete but failed to make it as a starting quarterback in the NFL. Jackson had incredible speed but the concern was he would not gel in a pro-style offense and did not have the passing accuracy to squeeze it in between NFL defenders, something you have to do on a regular basis to be a successful quarterback in the highest echelons of the NFL.

But coach John Harbaugh of the Ravens took a chance on Jackson early in the draft and decided to adjust his offense around him. The Ravens had Joe Flacco at the time, a veteran who was the complete opposite of Jackson, but once they put Jackson in the starting offense, the Ravens became more of a spread team with a passing attack. Jackson proved doubters wrong who did not think he could be successful as a starting quarterback in the NFL.

Coach John Harbaugh has fallen in love with Jackson and told him just how big an impact he has made on and off the field. In a conversation that was caught on tape after the team's 49-13 win over the Bengals in November 2019, Harbaugh sat next to Jackson and praised him. "Most quarterbacks worry about their stats, but you're a leader," Harbaugh told Jackson. "I love the way you play. You don't flinch, you just attack. All you do is attack. You changed the game, man. Do you know how many little kids in this country are going to be wearing No. 8 playing quarterback for the next 20 years?"[iv]

It was a poignant moment and a special one for Jackson. To have a Super Bowl-winning coach believe in him like that meant a lot. Jackson only looked back at Harbaugh and said, "And we're going to keep it going."[v]

We, not I. "We're going to keep it going." That is who Jackson is. He is team first all the time. He is not about ego. He is not about stats. He is about wins. He is about helping his team any way he can, lifting them up when they are down.

His record thus far as a starting quarterback in the NFL proves he is very successful at that.

Chapter 1: Early Childhood

Early Tragedy

Lamar Demeatrice Jackson Jr. was born on January 7, 1997, in Pompano Beach, Florida to Felicia Jones and Lamar Jackson, Sr. He is one of four children, growing up with a brother and two sisters. While Jackson is a star now and as rich as can be, his childhood was anything but easy or rich. Jackson and his family struggled with poverty and had to fight hard to make it in life. Without his mother, he said he would never have become a professional football player.

Lamar Jackson, Sr. was a big influence in Lamar's life early on. Young Lamar was described as a "daddy's boy" growing up. He idolized his father. He wanted to be like him. The two had an extremely close relationship, despite the financial struggles. Lamar, Sr. began coaching his son at a young age, throwing the football with him and helping him get faster. By the age of eight, Lamar could outrun many high school track athletes.

Lamar says he does not have a lot of memories of his father growing up, but he remembers his father playing with him and his siblings in the yard, always giving them advice and coaching them up.

Then came the worst day of Lamar, Jr.'s life. It would be the worst day of anyone's life. The family got a phone call that 31-year-old Lamar, Sr. had been in a car accident and died instantly. The death sent shockwaves through the family. And as if that was not bad enough, Lamar's grandmother, perhaps struggling to cope with the news of her son, died of a heart attack on that same day. Lamar had lost his role model, his father, and his grandmother, with whom he was extremely close with, in a matter of hours.[v]

Felicia Jones told them "not to cry; they would do better and amount to something." It was a turning point in Lamar's life. From then on, he went from being a "daddy's boy" to a "mama's boy." His mom would have the most tremendous impact on his life. Whoever thinks women cannot coach football should talk to Lamar, as his mother would become his greatest coach from that point on.[vi]

Mama Knows Best

A lot of people helped me get better when I was young, but the best coach I've ever had was also my first one: Mom. And I'm not saying that just because she looked out for me and encouraged me to pursue football and all that stuff. I mean she actually made me grind to get better."[v] - Lamar Jackson

Coaches are not just there for you in sports. They are there for you in life. When you go through tough times, they lift you up and point you in the right direction. When they see talent in you, they try and maximize it and help you achieve success. When you need someone to look up to for guidance, they are right there.

For Lamar Jackson, this was his mother. From the time his father died, Felicia Jones knew she had a colossal task—she had to raise a family on her own and work towards helping her children be successful in life. She had seen Lamar play football with his dad and witnessed the talent he had. He was fast and had incredible athleticism for such a young boy and she wanted him to explore that even further. She not only worked with him on the field, but she also recruited others to help him continually get to the next level.

When Lamar was eight years old, after his father had passed, he began to dislike football. However, Jones knew he could be amazing if he got a little push and began to like it again. She signed him up to play. In his first youth game, he scored two touchdowns and outran everyone on the field. After that day, football became his passion once again and Jones would help guide him in the right direction and set him up for success. That is what good parents do. They see the best in you and help you achieve your best.[viii]

Shortly thereafter, Jones found a coach that she thought would be perfect to train Lamar. McNair Park in Pompano Beach was really where it all began for him. There, Felicia Jones linked Lamar up with Van "Peanut" Warren, a youth football coach who specialized in helping train young quarterbacks. With Felicia watching, Warren ran Lamar through heavy drills and training every Sunday from 2 until 6 p.m. He ran sprint after sprint and was put through a long series of agility drills, all of this done without ever touching a football. He wanted to get Lamar in shape first before they worked on the technical part of football.[vii]

When it came to playing quarterback, Lamar sat on a metal bench and intently watched Warren, who simulated different quarterback drills for him. Jackson would take mental notes and then go home and work on those drills with his mother and his brother, Jamal. They all put on their equipment–even his mother.

"People don't believe me," Jackson said in an interview., "but she was an athlete. She used to play basketball. She saw what we were able to do, and she'd go back there and play football with us. She even got out there and tackled me. She was just making us tougher because she is older, so she is bringing power that we're not used to feeling. We didn't take it like anything different."[vii]

Many say that Lamar's eighth year was a rollercoaster. He had lost his grandmother and father in the same day and had lost his motivation to play football, but re-discovered it when his mother took him under her wing and began putting him through training to become not just a good football player, but a great one.

But to be great in football where Lamar was from, many times you had to be better than great. The thing about Florida, especially South Florida, is that it is very competitive. Athletes are born and raised there and some of the best college football coaches in the country swarm to places like Pompano Beach to watch young kids play. There are a lot of players just like Lamar who are fast, physical, and athletic. To be the best, you need to work harder than anyone else and have special talents that no one else can match. Many of the fastest athletes in the pros today came from Florida. It is a recruiting hotbed.

Most of these Florida stars, however, end up as running backs, defensive backs, or receivers because of their speed and size. Quarterbacks are a rare breed. Lamar had so many great qualities as a young athlete. Many thought he would be a wide receiver because of how fast he was, but Warren saw a chance for Lamar to transcend football at a young age. He saw qualities similar to Michael Vick in him but with more potential. His mother agreed and wanted him to play the position he most desired, which for Lamar was quarterback.

"She never let him change his position," Warren said. "The work ethic came from her."[vii]

Lamar had the drive inside of him. He worked harder than anyone at McNair Field and Jones was there to watch her son grow from a young boy with the potential to a future star. To be a star in Florida, you need to have that determination and motivation inside of you. Lamar had it. It went into overdrive before he was even a teenager.

Jackson actually became better at football by eluding his mom's tackles as he practiced at home. She would come after him, equipment and all, looking to tackle him, and he would learn how to avoid her. This was the start of something for Lamar. With the help of Coach Peanut and his mom's training at home, Lamar became faster and more elusive, the makings of a dangerous dual-threat quarterback in the future.

Jones took on the roles of both mom and dad when Lamar, Sr. passed away. She led her boys on fitness runs to get them into shape. Any time Lamar, Jr. wanted to end a workout with Warren, Jones would not allow it. She pushed him even harder than his coaches. She saw too much strength in him to have him ever give up, and her unflinching encouragement made Lamar stronger.

Most people hear the stories about how Lamar's mother was so aggressive with her son and do not believe it, not thinking she could play the game and push him the way she did. But Warren affirms that he saw it with his own eyes.

"It's all true," Warren said. "What's so remarkable about her is she took on the role of mother, father, and coach before she actually knew what she was doing. At the age of 7 and 8, you're just being a mom. She was the first one who was able to catch the ball with him. If they had a practice on tackling and mom's got to tackle, then mom's got to tackle. She knew with that gift, in order to be great, he had to put in the work."[viii]

It's unclear where Lamar would be today without his mother there to push him, as Warren said, but Lamar claims he definitely would not be in the NFL. He gained the passion to play from his father first, then his mother second. Coach Warren did a lot for his skills, but his mother's training at home took him to that next level, the level you need to be successful as an athlete in South Florida where the best of the best play.

"In towns like Pompano and Boynton Beach, there isn't much for young black kids to do," said Jackson's high school teammate, Tre'Quan Smith. "As far as football, your parents put you in it to get something out of it—to see if you can get a full scholarship, to motivate you and guide you with little small life disciplines that you learn. Football for us is a chance to make it out and support our families."[vii]

Football was life for Lamar as a child. He grew up in an apartment building just a couple blocks away from McNair Park, living in a low-income area of the city. Lamar said it was not a place most people would want to go visit. There were many bad things that happened there, from crime to drugs. Felicia kept Lamar focused, never allowing him to get in trouble or fall prey to the unsavory influences that surrounded him. She kept him focused on football.

Jackson also loved watching football on television. While he was a quarterback, he idolized Randy Moss and respected his dominance in the game. He also loved watching Miami Hurricanes football, especially the old school games when the team was a regular national championship contender.

"If I could go back and watch any event, I'd like to watch Sean Taylor live," Jackson said. "I'd like to watch those great Miami Hurricanes teams it was all of those guys like Ed Reed playing. That 2001 team, definitely."[xxxi]

That 2001 team was a favorite of anyone living down in South Florida. Some describe it as the greatest team ever assembled. It was not just Sean Taylor and Ed Reed. It was also littered with future NFL stars like

Vince Wilfork, Jonathan Vilma, Phillip Buchanon, Antrel Rolle, Willis McGahee, Clinton Portis, Frank Gore, Andre Johnson, D.J. Williams, and Jeremy Shockey. All these players went on to make Pro Bowls during their time in the NFL.[xxxi]

People who knew Lamar as a young boy described him as goofy with a bit of a charm. He was always kind and caring to others, but had that competitive edge about him when he stepped on the field. Friends and mentors called him "LJ" and said he was easy to get along with. He always had a smile on his face.[vii]

"He wasn't just like a friend; he was more like a brother," recalled Chauncey Mason, who played one season with Jackson growing up. "He took me in. If you ever got the chance to meet Lamar… he's just a very loving person."[vii]

When Jackson was in middle school, Jones moved the family about 30 minutes north and into Palm Beach County. There, he would not only play youth football, but he also practiced with Santaluces Community High School prior to going there his freshman year.

Lamar was not just all about football, though, as a child. Jones instilled upon her sons what she called "The Super 8," something Warren would carry on with his players. "The Super 8" was God, prayer, faith, family, education, sacrifice, character, and discipline. These things were all a big part of Lamar's life. They prayed and went to church, and she taught them the quality of being respectful and being disciplined. She also taught them the importance of family in life and how to always be there with them through good times and bad.[vii]

To this day, Lamar always prays to and thanks God for his mother, who played such a vital role in his life as a child. He also prays to his dad, who was also an inspiration in his life.

Jones took the boys to the beach all the time. Of course, there was always meaning to it. Yes, some of the time it was for fun, but other times, it was for work. She would make Lamar run in the sand with a parachute strapped to his back, a training exercise that would make Lamar faster. She also took Lamar to the beach to practice the drop-back technique in the sand, which helped with his form. She also ran Lamar and her boys through cone drills and worked with a medicine ball.

Lamar began to dislike the beach because of the misery and pain that Jones would put him through. "I won't lie, I used to complain a lot," Jackson said. "There were days I was like, 'Mom, I don't want to go today.'"[vii]

It did not matter how much Lamar complained. It did not matter how much he whined. It did not matter how much he begged not to go to the beach. They were going and he was working. From the age of eight until he graduated high school, Jones was constantly putting him through the wringer, never allowing him to quit on her or his teammates. The workouts got more intense and even more crowded as he got older. Once Lamar reached high school, his teammates often joined him on the beach with Jones as the coach.

"The workouts were intense," Tre'Quan Smith said. "My legs went numb. He does some extreme workouts with his mom. There's nothing easy that he does. The fundamental stuff, he's got that down pat so a lot of the stuff he works on is hard, like the stuff he has to do in games."[vii]

Jones kept coming up with creative ideas to train Lamar and his brother. One day, she bought a 300-pound tire and a sledgehammer. She had a couple of different purposes for them. First, she wanted her boys to be able to flip the tire all across the yard. She also wanted them to take the sledgehammer and pound the tire over and over. This worked on both cardio and muscle.[vii]

"What's interesting is Jones never had her boys do something she couldn't do," Warren said. "Yes, that meant she flipped the tire and pounded them with a sledgehammer, too."[vii]

A lot of coaches are like that because they want you to see that you are not alone. If they can do it, you can do it. It is a way of pushing them, and when that pushing is coming from your own mother, it makes it even more impactful.

The funny thing was, you could never spot Jones in the crowd. She always was the loud one on the field, but the quiet one in the stands and to the media. She never gave an interview or talked to the press. She wanted to be more behind the scenes. Whenever she watched Lamar play, she wore regular clothes and had her headphones on listening to gospel music, as she wanted to block out the noise and just focus on Lamar, making mental notes each time of things she sees him doing well and things he needs to work on. Then the next day, it was back to work.[vii]

"She still gives me advice today," Jackson recently said. "We'll talk about the game and she offers her critique. I take it seriously because she's still the most important coach in my life."[vi]

Coach Warren worked with Lamar all the way up until his high school days, preparing him for the next chapter in his life. After that, Joshua Harris became his regular quarterback coach and his mentor as he grew older. Warren and Jones were the perfect team to help Lamar and he used lessons from both coaches to improve himself to become one of the best players South Florida ever saw. His mom pushed him to no end, wanting Lamar to achieve things that no one else had ever achieved before.

"That's my mom, and she wanted to see me be great," Jackson said. "She said, 'If you want to do this, you're going to be great at it.' That's what I want to be, too. We have the same mindset."[vii]

Chapter 2: High School Career

Lamar Jackson's high school career did not exactly take off the way he wanted it to. Whereas many star quarterbacks excel from their freshman season, Lamar's did not truly materialize until his junior year.

When Jones moved her family north about 30 miles to Palm Beach County, Lamar initially enrolled at Santaluces Community High School, where he had already been working out since he was in middle school, hoping to make an impression. However, Jackson did not get the playing time he wanted to. He played sporadically during his freshman year, making the highlight reels when he did play, but then did not play at all as a sophomore. Instead, he spent it on the bench.[ix]

While Lamar never publicly admitted it or complained, there was frustration that the team would not guarantee him the starting quarterback job moving forward and he was splitting playing time his freshman year and in practices his sophomore year. Many who saw Lamar play thought he was undoubtedly the best quarterback at the school; to not be guaranteed the starting position deflated him and it also angered his mother.[x] He looked at transferring schools during the end of his sophomore season, which in South Florida, is actually quite normal. Many great athletes look to move to a better school for their career.

Rick Swain, the head coach at Boynton Beach High School, who had wanted Lamar, said his decision to transfer and come to his school "was a gift from the football gods."[x]

Lamar was impressed with Swain as a coach and the offense they ran there, realizing it fit his style of play perfectly. Swain had run the T-wing option, which is a type of spread offense that relies on quickness at the quarterback and wing positions, similar to what the college military academies run. Swain was constantly looking for speed at quarterback and he had converted a wide receiver on his team to run the offense and was grooming him at the time when Lamar arrived.

But that all changed on the first day of spring practice. Lamar, by then, had transferred to Boynton Beach, just in time to begin working with the team in April and May. Swain made a slight adjustment, wanting to see how Lamar would run a regular read-option play with no wingbacks, more typical of what you see in the college football system. He put one running back behind Lamar in the shotgun set and added more wide receivers to spread out the opposing side. Lamar took the snap, read the defensive end perfectly, and kept the ball. He then sprinted up the field 60-yards untouched, swerving his way around tackles along the way. Swain saw everything he needed to see immediately.

"Man, we're changing offenses," Swain remembers telling his assistant coach. "I've run this offense off and on for 20 years, but that ain't what we need to be running with this kid."[x]

Immediately, Boynton Beach switched their philosophy. Swain's plan was to tailor the offense to Jackson's strengths. Gone was the T-wing option and implemented was a pistol formation with four wide receivers. The plan? Spread defenses out just like he did in that play and let Jackson shred them up and down the field.

Swain recalls players' jaws dropping when they watched Lamar run in the offense. He was so fast, but even more impressively, he could throw. He was the high school version of Michael Vick. He could throw the ball 50 yards down the field on a rope while also having the ability to make tacklers miss left and right with his legs.

But while Jackson was making highlights with his arm and legs, it was the other side of him that was most impressing coaches and teammates. Jackson was a bona fide leader, and it was something that Swain said he saw in Lamar instantly. He listened intently and showed the utmost respect every time coaches approached him. Jackson was simply following his mom's "Super 8" model that she taught him, which included character and discipline. She had brought him up to be an elite young man destined for success.

The more Jackson played, the more colleges began to take an interest. But they were not sure what to make of him. He was so fast that coaches thought maybe he would be best suited to be converted into a wide receiver, a running back, or a safety. Lamar, however, would never change, and his high school coaches made sure to tell any college coaches that inquired about him that he was a quarterback first and always. Lamar's mother was also adamant that Lamar never went to a school that even considered changing his position.

One of the coaches who played a key role in Lamar's future was Lamar Thomas, a former standout at the University of Miami and an NFL player. Thomas played at Boynton Beach and was coached by Swain, and the two constantly kept in touch. In 2013, Thomas was coaching wide receivers at Western Kentucky under Bobby Petrino and eventually moved to Louisville when Petrino accepted a head coaching job there. Thomas was trying to help Swain sell Jackson to Petrino.

"His highlight film at first was runs and then throws," Thomas said. "I told [Swain], *'Hey, put that throwing on his highlight film first. Don't put that running crap up first'.*"[x]

When Petrino saw the film, he was floored. He asked Thomas whether he could get this kid. Thomas responded, "I got him."[x]

While all that was going on, Lamar was putting on a show on the field. In 2013, Jackson started nine games for the Boynton Beach Tigers. He threw for 1,264 yards while also running for 960 yards. He compiled a total of 29 touchdowns, a school record. 19 of those touchdowns came through the air while 10 were on the ground.

"He was a hard worker who was dedicated towards getting better," Swain said. "He was constantly improving his accuracy and decision-making."[x]

Jackson also got feedback from his mom, who was there at every game giving him advice. She kept working with him in the offseason, continuing to take him to the beach along with about a dozen of his teammates who had heard of Jones' workout program and wanted to join in.

Lamer continually improved throughout his high school career and he made Boynton Beach a legitimate state contender. Swain's football teams had a mix of good and bad teams over his tenure, but in the two years that Jackson was there and started, the team went 21-4 and outscored opponents by an incredible 536 points. In his two seasons as a starter, Jackson put up

2,246 passing yards, 1,624 rushing yards, and compiled 53 total touchdowns.[xi]

"As a coach, he really was the first kid that you were actually afraid of," said Jessie Hester, a former NFL player who coached against Lamar Jackson. "You just knew that this kid was better than pretty much all the guys you had on your team. You would just try to make sure that you kept the score at a respectable point."[xi]

Other coaches, like Hester, shared similar sentiments, knowing that when you faced Lamar Jackson, you were in for a tough match. There was no solution to containing him. Even if you shadowed him and ganged up on him running the football, he could kill you with his arm, which was just as scary. Hester once thought he had come up with the perfect game plan to stop him and spent a week's worth of time staying up at night working on his strategy to slow Jackson down. All the work he put in and all the optimism he had ended up crushed in defeat as Boynton Beach beat Hester's team 64-29.[xi]

"We tried to box Lamar in by trying to spy on him, not really rush him, and just hold the rushing lanes and keep him in the pocket," Hester said. "He was just so crafty that even though we were trying to spy on him, once he tucked it and went, we just didn't really have kids athletic enough to deal with what he brought to the table."[xi]

"I played him twice in a matter of three or four months," Village Academy coach Don Hanna said. "It didn't help a lot. We were better prepared, but the kid was such a dynamic player that two people could have him cornered and he'd find a way to get out of it."[xi]

Jackson had a lot of highlight plays in high school, but there was one specific play that stood out over others and went viral, making him a YouTube star. He was lined up in the shotgun in the red zone. He took the snap and quickly stepped forward to elude a hard-charging edge rusher. Without any throwing options downfield, he rolled to his right, pump-faked at the line of scrimmage, and then darted for the end zone. He pointed at a Village Academy defender while beating him to the edge and then shot up field like a bullet. Then, as another defender came flying in to stop him at the goal line, he abruptly stopped. He just hit the brakes. As the defender flew by him, Jackson just walked into the end zone and threw his hands in the air.[xi]

"During the moment, I didn't get a good picture of it, but just knowing that we had two people to, at worst, just knock him out of bounds and he was still able to stop on a dime, juke them and get in the end zone, that was a 'wow' moment," Hanna said. "That is the 'Lamar Jackson: Welcome to the World' clip."[xi]

Jackson was becoming increasingly popular as a high school player because of just how many video clips there were out there of him. Hudl was a platform where high school coaches could put together highlight reels and share them with prospective college coaches, and Jackson was definitely getting some interest. Besides Thomas, other media helped Swain put together a package that would "wow" other coaches and schools.

"He was the most dynamic high school football player I've ever seen, and he still is to this day," former football coach and Fox Sports radio host Chris Kokell said. "I've seen really good runners, I've seen really good throwers, but I've never seen someone do both except for Lamar Jackson."[xi]

Kokell was one of those media figures closely connected with Swain who helped him put together his Hudl package to share with others. But while Jackson was putting together highlight packages, he was also helping his team make a run at the state title in 2013, something unheard of for Boynton Beach. They had a massive playoff game with the No. 3 team in the state,

Miami Central, a team that most experts thought would roll over Boynton Beach. However, Jackson made sure that did not happen.

Many say it was that game that truly put Lamar Jackson on the radar. He had some great highlights and games already, but doing it against Miami Central and their formidable defense was a different story. If he was able to shine against them, the doubters would stop doubting.

Miami Central was loaded on offense and defense and had a running back named Dalvin Cook who was nearly impossible to stop—yes, that same Dalvin Cook who is now one of the best running backs in the NFL on the Minnesota Vikings.

But while Cook shined against Boynton Beach, so did Jackson, who made play after play and stunned their head coach and players. Jackson threw for 237 yards and ran for 194, which included an incredible 72-yard touchdown run that was included in Jackson's ultimate highlight package.[xii]

However, Swain's defense just could not stop Cook, who ran for 116 yards and 4 touchdowns, including an 85-yard punt return. Miami Central never punted and won the playoff game, 55-37.[xii]

Committing to College

After Jackson's incredible junior season, it was time for him to look into where he wanted to play college football. Lamar Thomas was a step ahead of all the other coaches and wanted desperately to persuade Jackson to play for Bobby Petrino at his new school, Louisville.

Petrino was sold after watching Jackson's highlight film, but he was not the one that Thomas needed to persuade. Neither was Jackson.

It was Mama Jones.

"First time I met her, she gave me the stare of death," Thomas said with a chuckle. "But I talked about greatness, and Lamar and Felicia talked about greatness. So, we were all on the same page."[vii]

That first meeting with Thomas, Jackson, and Jones was a success. Jones wanted to ensure that Jackson would not be moved from the quarterback position. It was his position. If they even tried to move him, he would back out. Thomas assured Jones that they would keep him at quarterback and tailor the offense around his talent. Jones was impressed, but before she signed off on her son going to Louisville, she wanted to meet Coach Petrino and hear it from him.

The second meeting between Jackson, Jones, and Louisville was with Petrino present in her home. Petrino promised Jones that her son would only play quarterback and would have a chance to compete for the starting job as a freshman. Both Jackson and Jones were very impressed by Petrino and Thomas's presentation and were committed to Louisville.

"Just from being around the situation, to get Coach Petrino to say something like that, that was big. That was huge," Thomas said. "It was also him being a man of his word. It forced him to be a man of his word, and it was a good thing."[x]

Coaches make an impact. For Jackson, that meant two coaches, Petrino, and his mom. But for a player to accept a position at a top university, he needs to feel a comfort level not just with the school itself, but also with the coach. It is such an important quality. There needs to a connection, a spark of chemistry that gives you the confidence that it will work. Both Jones and Jackson trusted Petrino and the situation they were about to walk into.

Perhaps what was most impressive is who Jackson turned down to commit to The University of Louisville. He was getting offered scholarships from Florida State,

Ohio State, Nebraska, Auburn, Georgia, and South Carolina. But just before the start of the 2014 season, Jackson verbally committed to Petrino's team. According to *247Sports*, Jackson was ranked No. 9 among dual-threat quarterbacks in the nation and No. 34 among all high school players in Florida.[xiii]

Jackson would follow Teddy Bridgewater, who also had a ton of success as a dual-threat quarterback at Louisville. Bridgewater gave Jackson some advice prior to him signing and it helped aid Jackson in wanting to go to that school.

"(Jackson) saw the success that Teddy Bridgewater had (at Louisville), and Lamar is very similar to Bridgewater," Swain said. "Obviously, you can't say he's as good as Bridgewater—he was awesome—but they're very similar, and Lamar might, in fact, I know, he has more speed than Bridgewater did. It makes him a true dual-threat quarterback."[xiii]

Swain went on to call Lamar the best player he ever coached by a mile. To have that kind of respect from your head coach meant a lot, and Lamar was looking forward to starting the next leg of his life's journey at the University of Louisville—and his journey wouldn't stop there.

Chapter 3: College Career

It did not take long for Lamar Jackson to make an impression at practice and convince Bobby Petrino he had found his future starting quarterback. Competing with Reggie Bonnafon, now a backup running back in the NFL, and Kyle Bolin, Jackson stood out on his very first play in fall practice. Petrino called a read-option play for Lamar and it went just like it did in his first practice at Boynton Beach. He read the defensive end perfectly, kept the ball, and went 75-yards up the field with blazing speed for a touchdown. Any talk of sitting Lamar out his freshman season so he could learn the offense and better prepare was not going to happen.[x]

Bobby Petrino and quarterbacks coach Nick Petrino both agreed instantly on that first day of practice that Jackson was not going to be red-shirted, which is what teams do to give their players an extra year of eligibility and learn behind another quarterback or position player. He was ready to go his first year. But he was still too raw coming out of high school. They would not start him right away, but rather slowly give him more playing time throughout the year until he was ready to take the reins by himself.

Bonnafon would be the opening day starter against Auburn in the Chick-Fil-A Kickoff Game. Jackson did get the playing time as Petrino promised, but it was not the start to his college career that he had dreamed of. On the first play of the game, Petrino called a trick play. Jackson rolled out and escaped coverage, then heaved a pass into double coverage down the field. Before he knew it, he already had thrown his first interception of the season.[x]

The first person to come over to calm Jackson down was the man responsible for bringing him to Louisville, Lamar Thomas. "I told him to forget about it. He just looked up calmly and said, 'I'm good, coach. When can I get back in?'"[x]

When Jackson got his second chance, he took advantage of it. He played sparingly from the second quarter on and ended up making some outstanding plays with his legs. He ran for 100 yards and threw for 106 and almost helped the Cardinals overcome a 14-0 deficit to win the game. Instead, they came up just short, losing to Auburn 31-24.[x]

For much of the first half of the season, Petrino played musical chairs at quarterback. Sometimes it was Bonnafon, sometimes it was Bolin. Jackson would come in and change the pace from time to time. Jackson was making great plays but also making some mistakes. However, one thing was catching Petrino's eye: Jackson was working hard to improve.

It was the same thing that Swain had always noticed about Jackson. He was determined to get better and would do whatever it took to take his game to the next level and to where he could be a dominant force in college football and hopefully the pros. Jackson had been through the gauntlet already with his mom. She had taught him to never give up, to never accept just being okay. She had taught him that to be the best, you needed to work the hardest. Jackson was practicing harder than any player and pushing himself to be a college football star.

The biggest thing Jackson wanted to work on was his turnover ratio. Through five games, he had thrown for three touchdowns and ran for five more, but he also had thrown four picks and lost a fumble. In his sixth game of the year, he came in against Florida State and saw extended time in the second half. Jackson began to find some rhythm through the air, going 20-for-35 for 307 yards against the vaunted Seminoles defense. He threw three touchdowns but also threw a pick in a 41-21 losing effort.[xiv]

Jackson's playing time continued to increase that freshman season as Petrino followed through on his plan to not just get him in the game more, but reward his hard work in practice. One critique Petrino had for Jackson was to always look to pass first, run second, as he wanted to see more of his arm that freshman year. He wanted Jackson to be that true dual-threat and have teams respect his arm. Jackson began putting up some impressive performances through the air while not running as much. In a win at Wake Forest, Jackson threw two touchdowns while compiling a 73.1 passer rating.[xiv]

By the time the season finale came against Kentucky, Bolin was starting and Jackson continued to wait for his turn. With the Cardinals trailing 21-0, Petrino turned to Jackson and asked him, "LJ, are you ready?" Jackson looked at him with a determined look. "Coach, I was born ready."[x]

It was not your typical "Go in the game for a few plays" order. It was a "this is now your team" order. From that point on, Jackson never saw the bench again. He shredded the Kentucky defense, gashing them for long run after long run and mixing in some passes here and there. By the end of the game, Jackson had accounted for 316 yards of total offense, 186 of those on the ground, and 4 total touchdowns. The Cardinals had waged a stunning comeback to beat the Wildcats 38-24—and earned a bowl bid in the process.[x]

In the Music City Bowl against Texas A&M, Jackson continued to turn heads. Once again, he performed the read-option to perfection. Whatever nerves he had earlier in the season were gone. He torched the Aggies defense with his legs, running for an incredible 226 yards and two touchdowns in helping lead his team to a 27-21 postseason win.[xiv]

Players and coaches could see the potential that lay ahead with their team and Lamar Jackson. They were beginning to see something special. They were excited for the 2016 season, knowing that with Lamar behind center and many of their best players returning, they could make a run at a national championship. They had that much faith in him.

Historic Season

That offseason, Bobby Petrino gave Lamar Jackson the assurance he would be the starter when the team embarked on the 2016 season. Jackson had an outstanding spring practice that only cemented his stance as the team's No. 1 guy. That spring he focused on leadership and building strong chemistry with the rest of the team. At home, he worked with his mom, continuing to find ways to improve and make himself the best possible quarterback in 2016.

Lamar's major goal was to become the biggest dual-threat in college football, even bigger than Deshaun Watson, who was a Heisman Trophy candidate at Clemson. At the end of 2015, he had made it clear that he was one of the fastest, if not *the* fastest, quarterback in all of college football and was difficult to stop. But he wanted to become that same force as a passer. That included limiting his turnovers and becoming a more accurate thrower of the football. He worked hard that spring and summer with his coaches and his mom to prove to the college football world he was the best.

What made Jackson such a respectable athlete was just how good a listener he was. There was not one coach ever to say that the things they taught him went in one ear and out the other. He listened attentively, accepted criticism, and worked hard to correct any bad habits. That is what makes you a better athlete. It is not so much improving on your good qualities, it is learning from your mistakes and turning weaknesses into strengths. Jackson was determined to be as perfect a quarterback as he could possibly be, and the respect he showed towards his coaches and his focus on heeding their critiques set him firmly on that path.

The hype going into Jackson's sophomore season was crazy. The last time people had seen him on national television, he was running circles around the Texas

A&M defense and had the media stunned. When they all ran to the practice fields to see him in the spring, they were just as amazed as they watched Lamar improve before their very eyes. Petrino said that game against Texas A&M was huge because it not only put Jackson in the spotlight, it gave him and his team confidence to take their game to the next level. [xv]

In the team's opening game that season against a much lesser opponent in Charlotte, Jackson continued to shine and show off his dual-threat ability. He had shown his improvement in the passing game, throwing for 6 touchdowns against the defense and running for 119 yards and 2 more scores. Jackson scored 8 touchdowns in total—all in the first half! After a 56-0 halftime lead, the Cardinals emptied their bench and let Jackson rest. The Cardinals opened the season with a 70-14 win against the 49ers. [xiv]

For those who said he could not do that against a better defense, Jackson only shrugged it off and proved his doubters wrong. He threw for 411 yards and ran for 200 against Syracuse, including one of the plays of the year where he hurdled a Syracuse defender on his way for a touchdown. Following that, the Cardinals and Jackson faced No. 2 Florida State.[xiv]

Playing at home, Louisville was an underdog against the Seminoles, whose athletes were some of the best in the country. These were also guys that Jackson had played against in high school, including Dalvin Cook. The media did not expect Lamar to be able to run circles against this defense filled with speed and talent.

They were wrong.

Louisville ran the pistol-and-spread offense to perfection, and their speed on offense topped Florida State's speed on defense. Jackson confused the Florida State defense, throwing laser passes and taking off for big gains. In the end, Jackson threw for 216 yards and ran for 146 in helping the Cardinals destroy the second-ranked, highly favored Seminoles 63-21.

Through three games that season, Jackson had thrown for 913 yards and run for 464 yards. After a win over Marshall, Louisville was 4-0 and ranked No. 3 in the country. They next faced a tough task, though, the following week: The No. 5 Clemson Tigers on the road in primetime on ABC with Chris Fowler and Kirk Herbstreit announcing.[xv]

Clemson had their own superstar at quarterback in Watson, who had helped get Clemson off to a perfect start in 2016. Watson helped get his team off to a dominant opening against the Cardinals at home in Death Valley. He was outshining Jackson and got the Tigers out to a 28-10 lead at halftime.

But in the second half, Jackson played some of the best football of his career and made plays all over the field, willing the Cardinals back into the game with his arm, his legs, and sheer determination. Jackson engineered an incredible comeback, outscoring the Tigers 26-0 to give his team a 36-34 lead late in the fourth quarter.

However, Watson was able to put together a game-winning drive in the final minutes to lead Clemson past Louisville, 42-36. It was an unfortunate end to a thrilling ACC matchup for the ages. And even though Louisville lost, it was their emergent star quarterback that everyone was talking about. Jackson finished with 295 yards passing, 162 yards rushing, and 3 touchdowns, and had begun to be hailed by experts and the media as the leader for the Heisman Trophy.[xvi]

Jackson's continued spectacular performances helped cement his lead in that race. He led Louisville in running off five straight wins after that Clemson loss and thrust them back into the conversation for a college football playoff berth. One of those five straight wins came against Virginia, a game in which Louisville was projected to win with ease. But teams have letdowns and don't always play their best, and after scoring just 14 points through three quarters and trailing 17-14, the outlook was murky. Jackson was able to lead his team back to take a 24-17 lead, but

Virginia countered as they scored late and converted a two-point conversion to take the lead back 25-24 with just 1:57 left in the game.

With his team on their own 25-yard line, Jackson orchestrated a drive that will go down in Louisville Cardinals history as one of the best ever in team history. Using his arm and legs, Jackson led his team swiftly down the field and into position for a game-winning field goal. But Jackson wanted more. He hit wide receiver Jaylen Smith on a beautiful, postcard-perfect 29-yard pass that landed just over a defender's hands with just 13 seconds left to give Louisville the lead and the win over Virginia.[xvi]

Louisville struggled in their final two games, costing them a shot at the college football playoff. They lost a huge road game at Houston and then followed that with a loss to Kentucky. However, against Kentucky, Jackson ran for 171 yards and 2 touchdowns while also throwing for 281 yards and 2 touchdowns. In all,

Jackson had seven 100-plus yard games in 2016, running for more than 1,571 yards and throwing for 3,543 yards.[xiv]

Jackson became the first player in NCAA football history to eclipse 1,500 rushing yards and 3,300 passing yards in a single season. He beat out Watson and Oklahoma quarterback Baker Mayfield for the 2016 Heisman Trophy Award, becoming the first player in Louisville history to achieve the honor.[xv]

"For my teammates, this is an award for all of us," Jackson said when accepting the award. He later added, "It's an honor to have my mom here by my side and to share this with her. Losing my father and grandmother on the same day… my mom was a real soldier. Mom, I love you so much."[xv]

It was an emotional moment for Lamar Jackson, one of triumph and pride, but also a humble and reverent one. It was not about him. It was about all those who had helped him get to where he was. Jackson displayed the leadership and character in his speech that made him one of the most respected players in college football, calling it a "team trophy," not an individual one. His mom was part of that team.

Jackson lost his final game of that 2016 season in the Citrus Bowl against LSU, but it did not dampen the incredible year that he had had. He set an ACC record with 51 touchdowns total and shattered pretty much every Louisville quarterback record you could think of. As the 2017 season approached, Jackson began setting his eyes on bigger things—the NFL.

Preparing for the Draft

Lamar Jackson's junior season was likely to be his last, as he planned to tackle the NFL after the season ended. However, he still wanted to prove himself as an elite and improving quarterback in college football, something that would be hard to do after his Heisman winning season. Many players that return to college after their Heisman year struggle to maintain the same high level of play.

Jackson, however, would not let that happen. While he struggled to outshine Baker Mayfield of Oklahoma, he still continued to blaze his way through the season and got an invitation to New York for the ceremony at the end of the year, alongside Mayfield and Bryce Love from Stanford. In the end, Mayfield would win the Heisman Trophy that year.

Jackson actually eclipsed his numbers from 2016, passing for 3,660 yards and rushing for 1,601. He combined for 45 touchdowns and ended his college career with more than 13,000 total yards (9,043 passing yards and 4,132 rushing yards) and 119 total touchdowns. He broke 42 school records at Louisville, including most rushing yards and most touchdowns.[xiv]

Most years, his numbers would have won him a Heisman, but a couple of factors prohibited him from winning it for the second year in a row. For starters, the committee very rarely gives the award to the same player twice. Only Archie Griffin in the early 1970s accomplished that feat. Even Tim Tebow could not win it two years in a row. Secondly, Louisville's season as a whole was not as good as 2016 and it got buried some in the news. They lost four out of their first nine games, including blowout losses to Clemson and North Carolina State. Jackson, however, eclipsed his number of 100-yard rushing games from a season ago with 9 of them, including a 180-yard performance against Boston College where he also threw for 332 yards and amassed 5 total touchdowns.[xiv]

After the season, Jackson decided to enter the NFL Draft, skipping the team's bowl game to avoid any crazy injuries and prepare for the next level. However, getting drafted high was going to be a challenge. People saw too much Robert Griffin III in Lamar Jackson, another college player who had torched defenses with his speed and arm but struggled in the NFL, mainly because of his lighter body and injuries.

Jackson did not have the build of a Cam Newton and scouts thought he needed to bulk up some to be successful as a running quarterback in the NFL.

Another issue was how deep the draft class was with quarterbacks. Baker Mayfield, Sam Darnold, Josh Allen, and Josh Rosen were the talk of the offseason and all four were expected to go within the first 15 picks. Jackson's name was not even mentioned alongside those guys. He was considered second-tier. Jackson's scouting reports expressed concerns that he was a "one read, two read, run" quarterback and that "he looks too early to run instead of showing patience." There was also concern about his passing accuracy at the NFL level and his ability to squeeze passes into tight coverage.

Most draft experts projected Lamar Jackson to go somewhere in the second or third round, but the Baltimore Ravens did not let that happen. With their 32nd pick, the Ravens made a trade to move up into the first round and selected Jackson, instantly creating competition between him and starting quarterback Joe Flacco, who did not have the same speed and was getting past his prime at 33 years old.

Jackson, sporting a green Gucci suit, came out of the draft room in Dallas when he heard his name called and shook hands with commissioner Roger Goodell as he was handed a Baltimore Ravens cap.

"When my name finally got called, I was like, 'Man, I'm glad I wore this suit,'" Jackson said jokingly during a post-draft news conference. "Just an honor for the Ravens organization to believe in me. And all the teams that passed me up… there's a lot that's gonna come with that."[xvii]

Ravens coach John Harbaugh said he was sold on Jackson after seeing him in workouts and after talking to former head coach Mike Shanahan, who had designed an offense in 2012 around Robert Griffin III, a spread option made up of read-option runs and passes. That season, Griffin III won Offensive Rookie of the Year before an injury damaged his NFL future and ability to play at the highest level. Griffin is now a backup in the NFL with the Ravens.

"He's (Lamar) a freak of nature," Shanahan said in a phone interview during the first round. "If he was in the right system to utilize his skills and he continued to progress at the next level in the drop back [passing] game, then you've got somebody pretty special."[xvii]

It was how the NFL itself was beginning to change. The Seahawks had also found success with Russell Wilson by adjusting their offense around Wilson's strengths, using more option reads in their offense. To be successful in the NFL, many times it is tailoring to the quarterback, knowing what makes them excel and reach their potential, that helps you get there. Harbaugh was about to do that in the future with Jackson.

Chapter 4: NFL Career

Rookie Season

Prior to the 2018 season, John Harbaugh implemented two different offenses for the Baltimore Ravens. He had his regular offense that he had been running with Joe Flacco, a typical pro-style offense that suited the veteran's game. However, Harbaugh also implemented a more pro-style spread offense with some pistol plays in it, similar to what the 49ers and his brother, Jim Harbaugh, ran when they had Collin Kaepernick and what the Redskins ran with Griffin III. Harbaugh's goal was to get Jackson some playing time as the season progressed and confuse defenses with two completely different quarterbacks and offensive packages.

What helped make the process easy was Jackson's willingness to improve and develop. During training camp, Jackson was looking every bit like a first-rounder. Harbaugh and coaches worked with Jackson on improving his accuracy as a passer and illustrating patience and poise in the pocket, not looking to run too quickly. In the NFL, there are too many good linebackers who have the speed to track you down right away if they sense that you are going to take off every time.

Jackson and Flacco built up a friendship and mutual respect during their time with Baltimore, but they were also driven by competition with the other. Flacco wanted to keep his job, while Jackson wanted to show he was the future. In the end, it made the Ravens even better in 2018 and both quarterbacks would get a lot of playing time.

Flacco acted as a mentor for Jackson that 2018 season, helping him develop as the season progressed. He was not able to mentor him from a skills perspective since the two had completely different styles, but he was able to mentor him from a leadership and maturity perspective, teaching him how to manage the game and take the reigns as a starter.

Jackson also was able to get mentored by Griffin III, who was the backup under Flacco at the time and was helped by the Ravens' new second offense. He was able to help Jackson from a skills perspective and fostered his development as both a passer and a runner.

Jackson used Flacco's words of encouragement and helped illustrate during the 2018 preseason that he was going to be a force to be reckoned with. Through his first three preseason games, he led his squad down the field routinely against backups, making plays with his legs and feet. Each game, he continued to show improvement. By the last preseason game, he was starting against the Redskins while a majority of the regular starters sat. He displayed an impressive first half of dual-threat ability, going for 9-for-15 for 109 yards while also carrying the ball three times for 25 yards.[xviii]

Jackson's impressive training camp and preseason earned him the backup job behind Flacco. It did not take long for him to see action. The Ravens were blowing out the Bills on opening week behind a strong performance from Flacco, and with a 40-3 lead, Jackson saw a lot of playing time in the second half. He showed his playmaking ability with his legs, rushing 7 times for 39 yards while struggling a bit through the air, completing just 1 pass on 4 attempts. But it gave him the chance to get some added playing experience against starters for the first time.[xx]

Halfway through the season, Jackson saw playing time in every game, mostly being used as a runner. However, Flacco was struggling as the team's starter. The Ravens lost three straight games in October and early November to drop them to 4-5 and were on the outside of the playoff picture. Flacco was also hurt in the team's loss to the Steelers, and with a bye week approaching, Harbaugh decided to use the time to prepare Jackson to start in the upcoming game against the Bengals on November 18th.

It did not take long for Jackson to prove himself. On the team's opening drive, Jackson moved his team down the field with his legs and his arm, finishing the 11-play, 75-yard drive by handing it off to Alex Collins who took it in for a touchdown.[xxi]

As with any rookie, Jackson had his bad moments, too. He threw a poor interception on his first drive of the second half that resulted in a Bengals touchdown, putting the Ravens down 14-13. But Jackson stayed calm. Down 21-13 in the fourth quarter, Jackson burst out for a big run, putting the Ravens in scoring position. Gus Edwards finished off the drive, and after the two-point conversion, the game was tied.[xxi]

Then late, Jackson again led his team down the field, gashing the Bengals defense and setting the Ravens up for the game-winning field goal. Jackson won his first start and showed off his speed and dual-threat ability.

As a passer, he was 13-for-19 for just 150 yards, but as a runner, he ran 26 times for 119 yards. Welcome to the NFL![xxi]

Harbaugh stuck with Jackson even as Flacco's health improved, wanting to see what the rookie could do and how the team reacted. It only got better from there. Jackson won his next two starts, beating the Raiders and the Falcons by double-digits. While people still speculated about his passing numbers, as he threw just one touchdown and two interceptions in those games, they were encouraged and excited with his running. The Ravens were changing. They had become a team built on speed and were confusing defenses. Jackson ran 28 times for 146 yards and 2 touchdowns in those two wins as he improved to 3-0 as a starter.[xx]

As Harbaugh continued to commit to Jackson while Flacco was not 100%, Jackson did not want to leave Joe out of it. "Joe is still a part of the team," Jackson said. "It's his team still, just like it's mine. It's all of our team. We're brothers. We're here together, each and every day. We've been here since camp putting our life on the line. It's still his team, man—nothing changed."[xix]

Jackson continued to put the team first. He knew what Flacco was feeling, but he wanted him to know he had his back and it was just as much Joe's team as it was his. Joe was still the leader of this Ravens while Lamar was leading the offense at that time and helping them win games.

"Joe teaches me a lot, just from him being a Super Bowl-winning quarterback," Jackson said.

Rookie mistakes were common that first season. Jackson struggled at times to hold onto the football, and a key fumble late in a game against the Chiefs cost the Ravens the game. Jackson had experienced his first loss as a starter. But he rebounded by winning the final three games of the season, rushing for 224 yards and 2 touchdowns as he helped lead the Ravens to the playoffs and the AFC North title.

Under Jackson as the starter, the team was 6-1. He had transformed the offense and gave the Ravens reasons to be optimistic about the future. He was not only frustrating the opponents' defenses; he was dazzling fans. He was exciting to watch. The doubters did not think his game from college could transport into the NFL. He was proving them wrong.

In the team's Wild Card Game against the Chargers, Jackson continued to display his dynamic side as well as his rookie side. While Jackson was able to make plays with his arm and legs again, he fumbled three times, losing one of them. It was the biggest weakness that Jackson felt he needed to improve upon for the 2019 season.

Down 23-3 in the fourth quarter, Jackson propelled his team down the field twice, connecting with Michael Crabtree on two touchdown passes to cut the game to

23-17. However, a failed onside kick with under two minutes left deflated the Ravens Super Bowl hopes and their season ended at their home field.[xx]

Despite the sour taste of losing the Wild Card, Jackson took some huge steps forward in his career in 2018. Just a year ago, there were questions about whether he would even be a starting quarterback in the NFL. He started the season as the backup quarterback but was thrust into the starting position midway through, where he remained. Some draft gurus had projected him to not even go until the second or even the third round. He went in the first. Furthermore, he exceeded many people's expectations, going 6-1 and winning the AFC North.

Two people, however, were not surprised: Lamar and his mom. Felicia Jones knew Lamar had it in him to make it to the top level and succeed. She helped instill that same confidence in Lamar, who knew he had a lot more improving to do but never questioned his ability to do it. He could be, he *would* be, a special quarterback in 2019.

Indeed, he was and then some.

MVP Season

The team officially handed the reigns over to Jackson when they released Super Bowl-winning quarterback Joe Flacco in the offseason. By keeping Robert Griffin III as Jackson's backup, it signaled one system for the Ravens. It was all about moving at a fast-pace. They would be a run-first team, but that did not mean they would not throw.

One of the biggest question marks going into the new season was Jackson's arm. Many said he did not have the arm skill to take his game to the next level. Jackson was not about to accept that, however. He worked incredibly hard in the offseason and training camp to not just improve his turnover ratio, but also to improve his skills as a passer. The team drafted Marquise Brown and also tried to build chemistry between

Jackson and tight end Mark Andrews to make the Ravens a running and passing threat. Jackson knew Brown from his Pompano Beach days as they had played youth football together. Jackson worked with Andrews during the pre-draft workouts with coaches, who were watching to see whether he would be a good fit in the offense.[xxii]

It did not take long for Jackson to quiet his critics. In the team's opening game of the 2019 season, Jackson and the Ravens traveled down to Miami to take on the Dolphins. The Dolphins stacked the box, wanting to spy on Jackson, but instead were shredded through the air. Jackson flexed his arm to spectacular effect and only ran it three times all game. He connected on 17 of 20 passes for 324 yards and 5 touchdowns. He finished with an overall rating of 158.3, helping the Ravens bury the Dolphins 59-10.[xx]

"Not bad for a running back," Jackson tweeted after the game. The quote was an obvious poke at the media, who had labeled Jackson a runner, not a passer, and was a quote that became a trademark as his season progressed, even showing up on t-shirts.[xxiii]

At home against Arizona and Kyler Murray, Jackson picked up where he left off in Miami, this time using both his arm and his legs to completely dominate the Cardinals defense. Jackson ran for 120 yards while also completing 24 of 37 passes for 272 yards. Mark Ingram and Jackson decimated the Cardinals' run defense as the Ravens started 2-0, beating the Cardinals 37-24.[xx]

As the season progressed, several things were becoming clear. First, Jackson was throwing it a lot more and had improved on his accuracy. He was also turning it over a lot less and was still as dominant on the ground, making him an even bigger dual-threat to opposing defenses.

That entire season, Jackson had just three games where he threw an interception. After two losses to the Chiefs and Browns to drop the Ravens record to 2-2, it was what Jackson and his teammates did the rest of the season that caught the most attention.

Over his final 11 games that season (Jackson did not play in the team's finale), Jackson did not lose a game. He put up an incredible stat line that included a 66.1 percent completion rate. He threw 36 touchdowns, No. 1 in the NFL. He also topped the NFL in touchdown percentage. His touchdown-to-interception ratio was also the best, tossing 36 TDs while throwing just 6 picks all year. He was a clear No. 1 among all quarterbacks in rushing yards, tallying 1,206 yards for 7 touchdowns. He ranked No. 6 among all rushers in the NFL, the first quarterback in NFL history to finish with over 3,000 passing yards and 1,000 rushing yards in one season.[xxii]

The Ravens finished the season 14-2, meaning Jackson was 19-3 as a starter in regular-season games during his NFL career. They had run off 12 straight wins to close out the season. In his 15 games as a starter, Jackson had an 81.9 passer rating, five points higher than the second-ranked quarterback in that category. He broke Michael Vick's rushing record for a quarterback by 167 yards. Jackson ended with more rushing yards in 2018 than Saquon Barkley, Leonard Fournette, teammate Mark Ingram, Aaron Jones, Todd Gurley, Alvin Kamara, Melvin Gordon, and Le'Veon Bell. [xxii]

Many were calling Jackson the most elusive player since Barry Sanders. Jackson had five games where he ran for over 100 yards, including a stellar performance at home in the rain against the stout 49ers defense, ranked No. 2 in the NFL that year. He had three games where he tossed five touchdowns and had one game against the Bengals where he had accumulated a perfect 158.3 overall rating with an 88.2 completion percentage. It was his second game that season with a perfect passer rating, joining Ben Roethlisberger as the only other quarterback to achieve that feat. He gave spectators one of the most jaw-dropping highlights of the year, executing a spin move on his way to a 47-yard touchdown run that left defenders stunned.[xxii]

The voting for Offensive Most Valuable Player for 2019 was not even close. Jackson was a unanimous winner in a historic season. But despite the talk during the season of him winning the MVP, Jackson was focused on just one thing.

"I'm trying to win a Super Bowl," Jackson said. We're taking it a game at a time. I'm not worried about MVP."[xxiii]

That goal started in January against the Tennessee Titans but it would not have a happy ending. Despite being heavily favored, the Ravens ran into a team that was perhaps hotter than them, which is hard to believe. The Titans had just come off an upset of the defending Super Bowl champion Patriots at Gillette Stadium in Foxborough.

Jackson would throw for 365 yards and run for another 143 against the Titans, which most would believe would be enough to lead the team to an easy victory. But Jackson also threw two picks and lost a fumble, and the Ravens defense could not contain Derrick Henry, who dominated the game with 195 yards rushing on 30 attempts. Despite a lopsided stat line that saw the Ravens outgain the Titans 530-300, the Titans took advantage of Jackson's turnovers and the Ravens' inability to stop Henry, ending Baltimore's Super Bowl hopes with a 28-12 win on the road.[xx]

The Titans would go on to lose to the Chiefs in the AFC Championship, who in turn beat the 49ers in Super Bowl XLIV for their second-ever world championship.

For Jackson, it was a bittersweet season. He established himself as one of the best, if not *the* best quarterback in the game, and clearly illustrated that he was a true dual-threat player at that position by destroying defenses with his arm along with his legs. But after hardly turning the ball over all season, his three turnovers in the divisional round against the Titans were costly and his dreams of a Super Bowl had to wait.

"We just beat ourselves," Jackson said. "I had a lot of mistakes on my half; three turnovers, that shouldn't happen. They came out to play. We just started out slow. We've just got to do better next time, but [now it's] moving forward, get ready for this offseason, get ready for next year."[xxiv]

Good quarterbacks do that. They take responsibility for their mistakes and work towards getting better, even in challenging times. Jackson's struggles in early postseason games can be expected. After all, he was still just barely out of college. Success does not come overnight. His next step is clearly to perform just as well in the postseason as he did during the regular season, and if 2020 is any indication thus far, he will have another shot at it.

Jackson is not alone among quarterbacks who struggled early on in their careers in the postseason. Randall Cunningham threw five interceptions and no touchdowns in his first three playoff starts. Peyton Manning started his playoff career 0-3 with three dismal performances compared to his regular-season statistics. John Elway lost his first playoff game 31-7 and struggled and then lost 9-7 to the Steelers the following year after finishing 13-3 in the regular season. Aaron Rodgers, Dan Marino, and Drew Brees also had subpar performances and lost their first playoff games.[xxiv]

Looking at all those quarterbacks, some of the best in NFL history, Jackson should hold his head high. His career is just getting started and the Ravens are littered with young talent and look to be an every-year contender moving forward, especially with Jackson as the quarterback.

"I know how he's going to respond," head coach John Harbaugh said. "He's going to respond by being extremely motivated and determined to improve as a football player. The strides he made between last year and this year are pretty indicative of that, and we expect him to continue to get better. I just know his character and who he is as a person. That's what he'll be thinking about."[xxiv]

As the 2020 season pushes forward, Jackson continues to dominate games and be one of the winningest quarterbacks in his first three seasons of any that have come before him. Midway through the 2020 season, Jackson has an incredible regular-season record of 25-5 as a starter in the NFL.

He has already earned himself a Most Valuable Player Award and was named to the 2019 Pro Bowl Team where he won the MVP Award for that game.

Additionally, he was named Offensive Player of the Week six times in his first 23 regular-season starts as well as Offensive Player of the Month two times. He also won the FedEx Air Award, the Sporting News Offensive Player of the Year, and Bert Bell Award in 2019 and was ranked the No. 1 Player on the NFL Top 100 Players list in 2020, a designation chosen by fellow and former players.[xx]

Jackson has already set 28 Baltimore Ravens records and 31 all-time NFL records in just two years of playing time.

Despite the dual-threat ability he has displayed the first two seasons, Jackson continues to not see himself as a running quarterback. It is not his job and he has been quoted many times saying that his main job is to get it to the receivers and throw the ball, not run it. He only likes to run when he has to.[xxv]

Through his first two seasons, Jackson has also acknowledged that he has a lot of room for growth and he is trying to get better with each and every practice and every game. He does not stop working until he feels he has accomplished that. When asked what advice he would give to young athletes who get down on themselves and frustrated when they are not doing well, Jackson just smiled and responded, "Be happy. God gave you a breath to breathe every day. You don't need to be mad about nothin'."[xxv]

Chapter 5: Personal Life

People that know Lamar Jackson best, from his best friends to his football coaches, use a variety of words to describe him off the field. Some of those words include happy, quiet, private, low profile, funny, family, and religion. Of all those things, it is family that Jackson holds closest and dearest to his heart.

Many say Lamar is just like his mother, not wanting to be the focus of attention and trying to stay behind the scenes, although nowadays, that is pretty much impossible, given that he is the talk of the NFL for his playing ability. Jackson was described as someone who was never selfish, never wanting the attention. When he was given praise, he preferred it to be given to others, calling his wins "team wins" and always complimenting the players around him for their dynamic play, such as his offensive line.[xxvi]

While most people know about the impact his mother, Felicia Jones, has had on Lamar, most don't know about his brother and sisters, a group that Lamar thinks the world of and talks to every day. He credits them a lot for his success and they love him back.

"You make my life special," his brother, Jamar, said, choking up and wiping away tears as he touched on Jackson's rise from their backyard to the NFL. "Whenever you're away from me, I just always want to talk to you."[xxvi]

It continues to speak to the family bond the Jacksons have. They are one of the closest families anyone could find, and Lamar credits his mom for that as well as God. His brothers and sisters have said that the death of their father brought them closer together. It was such a difficult experience to bear, but they leaned on each other and that got them through the darkest time of their lives.

During the offseason, Jackson goes back to Pompano Beach frequently to help out his former quarterback coach, Joshua Harris. There he works with young quarterbacks and helps them develop and gives them advice on moving forward. On many trips, he brings teammate and wide receiver Marquise Brown with him, whom Jackson played Pop Warner football with and competed against in high school.

Felicia Jones and her family have upgraded their living facility since they were younger. Jones owns property in Owings Mills where Jackson also lives, an upscale living area where a lot of the wealthier people in Baltimore reside. Jones, who acts as her son's business manager, is about 20 minutes from the practice facility and goes to all of her son's home games as well as most away games.[xxvi]

It is easy to spot Lamar Jackson in the Owings Mills community as he is usually the sharpest dressed person there. Jackson has had an obsession with fashion since he was a young boy, leading him to even create his own company, Era 8 Apparel. The clothing line includes sweatshirts, T-shirts, tank tops, and fleece shorts. Much of the clothing has Jackson's number on it and even a catchy saying. Some of those sayings include, "Not bad for a quarterback" and "Action Jackson."[xxvi]

Jackson does not like to just go fast on the field, he has gotten a bit of a reputation for being fast behind the wheel as well. The most trouble he has gotten into in his life has been with speeding, even getting a ticket which made some headlines and led him to apologize for his behavior. But outside of speeding, Jackson has never been involved in any illegal activities, nor has he gotten in trouble for drugs or alcohol as many athletes do.

For fun, Jackson likes to spend time with his family and hang out with his friends, whether it be his current friends in Baltimore or his old friends in Pompano Beach. He spends time with his brother frequently and enjoys watching football and helping young athletes take their games to the next level.

Most have described Jackson as one of the more courageous men they have met. After all, to take hits every week from some of the strongest and hardest-hitting men in the country the way he does is not something to take on if you are not gutsy and fearless. Jackson, though, attributes his courage to his mother.

"I got it from becoming a man at such a young age," Jackson said in an interview. "My mother raised me on her own. All that came into play. I had to mature early."[xxxi]

Love Life

Jackson keeps his dating life very private and does not speak out much about it, but he does have a girlfriend, Jaime Taylor. The two have been dating for over three years now and have kept their relationship just the way Jackson and Taylor want it—very behind the scenes. The two met when Jackson was finishing up his playing days at Louisville.

According to Taylor, Lamar does a great job handling the noise around him and blocking out criticism. While it frustrates her any time the media picks on her boyfriend, he handles it just like he does moments on the football field: He shrugs it off and moves on. He just blocks it out, very similar to how his mom blocks out the noise during games by listening to gospel music.

"He's taught me how to handle criticism," Taylor said in an interview with *BaltimoreRavens.com*. "I mean, I used to get mad when I'd read stuff. Then I'd look at him, and he's just fine. He says, 'Let them do the talking. You don't have to say anything. Just show them.'"[xxvii]

Taylor is a huge Harry Potter fan and even got her boyfriend to dress up as Harry Potter for Halloween in 2019. Lamar posted a photo of himself on Instagram wearing the popular Gryffindor robe and Harry Potter glasses.

"Yes, I was Harry," Jackson chuckled. "I thought it was pretty cool. My girl she wanted [to do a Harry Potter theme]. Had the little coat on, I felt like I was back at the wizard's place. It was pretty dope...I wouldn't say I am [a fan of Harry Potter]."[xxvii]

Like any good partner, Jackson has tried hard to accommodate his girlfriend and make her happy. He has stayed up late watching Harry Potter movies with her, but Jackson has said he keeps falling asleep every time it comes on.

Personal Interests

Jackson's type of movies includes more drama and action. He is not nicknamed "Action Jackson" for nothing. He is old school when it comes to television shows, preferring to watch "The Fresh Prince of Bel-Air," "The Jamie Foxx Show," and "The Wayans Bros." Jackson even turns on old school cartoon shows once in a while.[xxxi]

When It comes to music, Jackson always listens to Kodak Black before games as well as NBA YoungBoy, Young Thug, and Future. Jackson is also a fan of 21 Savage and attended one of their concerts while he was at Louisville. Interestingly enough, Jackson actually knows Kodak Black personally, as the two of them have a bit of a past together.

"Yeah, we're from the same neighborhood. We just went to elementary school together. He was doing his thing. I was doing mine."[xxxi]

Jackson's Endorsements and Charities

For a long time, Jackson held off signing any endorsement deals, instead propping up his Era 8 Apparel company. But in August 2020, he inked a contract with Oakley, even wearing an Oakley football shield on his helmet. He joined JuJu Smith-Schuster, Derwin James, and Patrick Mahomes, who also have deals with Oakley. Jackson has even advertised Oakley sunglasses in recent months.[xxviii]

Jackson has a $9.7 million salary with the Ravens and, as of August 2020, has a total net worth of $4 million. That number is likely to skyrocket in the coming months and years as Jackson signs more endorsement deals. He was recently put on the cover of the latest Madden '21 video game, which is extremely popular, given that the PlayStation 5 and Xbox Series X was just released.[xxviii]

Jackson has not yet gotten far enough into his career to start his own charity, but it is something he has said he wants to do as his career develops. That has not stopped him, however, from donating to other charities. In January 2018, Jackson donated $29,000 to charity, $25,000 of which went to Blessings in a Backpack. His money was raised by him signing autographs for young children and donating the money to charity. The program helped feed 90,000 students nationwide.[xxix]

Over the past year, Jackson has visited black communities and helped those who have fallen on tough times. The city of Baltimore has endured a lot of hardships in recent years with many families struggling to make ends meet.[xxx]

Jackson recently partnered with Lowe's and The Southwest Partnership to help give support towards The United Way Center in a historic neighborhood in Southwest Baltimore. His hopes are to give a large sum of money to build massive improvements to the center, such as new education and daycare resources and recreational areas for children.

"It's just a dream of mine, ever since I was a little kid, to be able to give back to the communities," Jackson said. "And for Baltimore to believe in me and have me as their starting quarterback, it was only right for me to go down into a neighborhood... and give back to the community."xxx

Jackson is one of 32 players in the NFL participating in the Lowe's "Home Team" initiative, which will also assist with housing repairs and building projects in the town he chooses, which happens to be Baltimore. He will also donate money towards disaster recovery and veterans' assistance.

"Any opportunity that I have to give back to Baltimore," Jackson said, "I'm proud of that."xxx

Jackson has continued to illustrate the caring, kind, and humble person he is, even as fame has come his way. He is quickly becoming a role model for children everywhere. Through good times and in bad, Jackson has always wanted to lend a helping hand and share his smile with those who are not as fortunate. He has taken an initiative to help those hurt by the recent social injustice crimes and pledged his support for anyone who needs it. He has always said he just wants everyone to be happy and the world to be a better place. Human beings like Jackson make us realize there is a lot of good in this world.

Chapter 6: Legacy and Future

Lamar Jackson has already cemented his legacy in the NFL at a young age, breaking dozens of records and helping change the game for future generations. John Harbaugh's ability to tailor his offense to Jackson's strengths and to watch it work the way it has is already leading to more coaches following suit.

Joshua Harris, one of Jackson's early quarterback coaches, said what the Ravens did set a standard for other teams to follow.

"I was like, 'Wow, they already know how to use Lamar,'" Harris said. "That intrigued me. After that day, my leader in the clubhouse was the Ravens." He continued, "Other organizations might have tried to mold Lamar into what they wanted him to be. The Ravens, though, molded their offense around Lamar."[xxv]

It is how teams sometimes fail with quarterbacks. They try to force their system around them instead of adjusting their system around what works for the quarterback. Kliff Kingsbury has a similar weapon in Kyler Murray, another former Heisman Trophy winner. In 2019, Kingsbury used Murray sparingly as a runner but watched Lamar Jackson destroy teams with his legs, helping transcend the position to a new level. Kingsbury has since used some of that philosophy from Harbaugh and Jackson and it has worked in 2020 for Murray. After running it just 93 times for 544 yards in 2019, Murray has already eclipsed that in just 10 games in 2020. He has 92 rushes for 619 yards and is on pace to become the third-ever quarterback to surpass 1,000 rushing yards in a season, joining Jackson and Michael Vick.[xxxii]

The difference between Jackson and Murray, as opposed to Vick, is the offenses being run. Both Harbaugh and now Kingsbury are bringing some of the college system over to the pros while Vick and other speed quarterbacks before him ran a pure pro-style offense. And there is more to come. Brian Flores of the

Miami Dolphins is already using Tua Tagovailoa in a similar way as he is just getting his NFL career started. Next year, Justin Fields of Ohio State and Trey Lance of North Dakota State will enter the 2021 Draft and bring some of the same traits as Jackson and Murray, dual-threat quarterbacks with explosive qualities.

Jackson has proved it can work and become a trendsetter in that regard. The spread option and pistol option can succeed in the NFL with the right guy to lead the offense, and if it continues to succeed in years to come, Jackson will be the Godfather of it all. He will have helped transcend the game in a way no one else has.

Besides becoming the first-ever quarterback to reach 3,000 passing yards and 1,500 rushing yards in his first two seasons (along with some of the other records we mentioned earlier), Jackson also owns many more records that will be difficult to break over the coming years, some of which are even through the air, not the ground. He is the only quarterback to ever throw 4 passing touchdowns and have 50 rushing yards in consecutive games. He is the youngest player ever with multiple five-touchdown performances. He also holds the NFL record for most consecutive 60-plus rushing yard games with 9, a record he broke in 2019. Of course, the previous holder just happened to be himself when he did it in 2018 and again in 2019.[xxxiii]

And there is more. Jackson is the youngest quarterback to ever start in a Pro Bowl game and followed it up with being the youngest player ever to win Offensive Pro Bowl MVP in 2019. Jackson is the fastest player to ever reach 5,000 passing yards and 2,000 rushing yards and holds the all-time record for most games with three touchdowns or more in a season with eight.[xxxiv]

Some of those records may someday be broken because of the transcendence of the game itself, which he helped set in motion. Over time, more running quarterbacks with speed and accuracy will enter the game and aspire to be just like Jackson. However, Jackson's goal is to keep moving forward. He is not focused so much on leading the new era in the game, he is focused on getting better and helping his team win a Super Bowl. Many great quarterbacks have come before him and set records of their own, but what means more to them all than those records is the ultimate prize? A Super Bowl ring.

"They're gonna get a Super Bowl out of me," Jackson told the Ravens the day he was drafted in 2018.[xxv] The Ravens are definitely in the conversation as they appear headed for their third straight postseason in 2020. The same teams, though, will always be an obstacle that Jackson will have to get past: The Chiefs, the Steelers, the Ravens, and the Patriots. All four teams seem to have Jackson's number, and for Jackson to get to the next level, he and his team will have to find a way to get past those franchises in the playoffs.

Jackson is also proof that you do not have to be a top quarterback in the draft to excel in the pros. In 2018, he was a second-tier pick and went even sooner than many originally thought he would or even deserved. He was not among the top group of guys, and trust me, many teams who passed him up are probably rethinking those decisions. Lamar Jackson is proving to quarterbacks coming out in the draft that you can still be a Most Valuable Player at quarterback despite not being the most sought-after college player. Others have also come before him and proven that very same thing, including an unathletic guy named Tom Brady who went in the sixth round in 2000.

Jackson hopes he is setting an example for young athletes everywhere, proving that no matter what obstacles are thrown your way early in life, you can still achieve your dreams. Jackson did not grow up rich. He did not grow up lucky. He has worked very hard for everything he has accomplished. And he played a position that was not typical of a black player in South Florida. His most influential coach was his mom.

Jackson always had the right attitude and disposition. Despite all the difficult things that happened early on, he never got down on life. His mom would never let him do that. His family leaned on each other. Lamar stayed positive, and when things got tough, he got tougher. He learned early on the importance of family, and furthermore, he learned that everyone out there on the field with you every day is not just your team. They are your family, too. They are your brothers in arms. You lean on them in good times and in bad. You raise them up when they get down, and they do the same for you.

The lessons that Jackson learned as a child continue to resonate with him today, and because of that as well as his extraordinary talent, a Hall-of-Fame berth is very likely awaiting him in the future.

Conclusion

Thus far in 2020, Jackson has given no indication he is letting up. He continues to shine as a dual-threat quarterback that defenses must game plan around and worry themselves about. Experience is playing a major role in making Jackson better, not just at quarterback, but as a leader of the team. He and Patrick Mahomes have built a bit of a rivalry in the AFC that is likely to carry on for many years to come. Some even say it is the next Tom Brady-Peyton Manning rivalry in the NFL.

Jackson hopes to one day top Mahomes, just like Manning eventually got past Brady. It took several years, but Manning got his rings. Jackson needs to continue to be patient and focus on improving as a player, on and off the field. With time will come continued success and eventually a championship ring.

When it comes to role models in the NFL, Jackson stands out alongside Mahomes as one of the most revered and respected in the game. You hardly ever hear anyone say a negative word about Jackson, especially as a person.

Part of the reason why Jackson is such an asset in the league is because of where he landed. We've heard this with guys like Tom Brady and Russell Wilson—if they landed on another team with another system, they very possibly might not be the quarterback they have become.

"He could have gone to another team and not nearly be the quarterback he is now," former Louisville offensive coordinator Mike Summers said of Jackson. "It's to the Ravens' credit that they understand that Lamar can make their team into a championship team, while other teams might try to make Lamar into their kind of quarterback instead and limit their chances."[xxxv]

The chemistry that Jackson has built with Harbaugh is special, and it often takes that special relationship to build a true championship quarterback. Belichick had it with Brady. Carroll has it with Wilson. Reid has it with Mahomes.

"Coach Harbaugh showed he was all-in [during that playoff game], and Lamar loved that," Harris said. "Lamar's biggest thing is loyalty, and he loves to see his loyalty reciprocated. The greatest thing I've seen from Coach Harbaugh is he's bought into who Lamar is. Any time I talk to Lamar about him, he talks about him in an endearing way. He is *Harbs*. He is a person Lamar feels has his back."[xxxv]

Having that relationship with your coach is so important for a young athlete. It makes you want to play. It gives you that fire inside. It makes football fun, not miserable. It brings the locker room closer together and gives you a future to look forward to.

For Lamar Jackson, that future is now looking as bright as ever. Five years from now, more young athletes out there will want to wear number 8 and say "I want to be like Lamar Jackson when I grow up.

Final Word/About the Author

I was born and raised in Norwalk, Connecticut. Growing up, I could often be found spending many nights watching basketball, soccer, and football matches with my father in the family living room. I love sports and everything that sports can embody. I believe that sports are one of the most genuine forms of competition, heart, and determination. I write my works to learn more about influential athletes in the hopes that from my writing, you the reader can walk away inspired to put in an equal if not greater amount of hard work and perseverance to pursue your goals. If you enjoyed *Lamar Jackson: The Inspiring Story of One of Football's Star Quarterbacks,* please leave a review! Also, you can read more of my works on *David Ortiz, Mike Trout, Bryce Harper, Jackie Robinson, Aaron Judge, Odell Beckham Jr., Bill Belichick, Serena Williams, Rafael Nadal, Roger Federer, Novak Djokovic, Richard Sherman, Andrew Luck, Rob Gronkowski, Brett Favre, Calvin Johnson,*

Drew Brees, J.J. Watt, Colin Kaepernick, Aaron Rodgers, Peyton Manning, Tom Brady, Russell Wilson, Odell Beckham Jr., Bill Belichick, Charles Barkley, Trae Young, Gregg Popovich, Pat Riley, John Wooden, Steve Kerr, Brad Stevens, Red Auerbach, Doc Rivers, Erik Spoelstra, Michael Jordan, LeBron James, Kyrie Irving, Klay Thompson, Stephen Curry, Kevin Durant, Russell Westbrook, Anthony Davis, Chris Paul, Blake Griffin, Kobe Bryant, Joakim Noah, Scottie Pippen, Carmelo Anthony, Kevin Love, Grant Hill, Tracy McGrady, Vince Carter, Patrick Ewing, Karl Malone, Tony Parker, Allen Iverson, Hakeem Olajuwon, Reggie Miller, Michael Carter-Williams, John Wall, James Harden, Tim Duncan, Steve Nash, Draymond Green, Kawhi Leonard, Dwyane Wade, Ray Allen, Pau Gasol, Dirk Nowitzki, Jimmy Butler, Paul Pierce, Manu Ginobili, Pete Maravich, Larry Bird, Kyle Lowry, Jason Kidd, David Robinson, LaMarcus Aldridge, Derrick Rose, Paul George, Kevin Garnett, Chris Paul, Marc Gasol, Yao Ming, Al Horford,

Amar'e Stoudemire, DeMar DeRozan, Isaiah Thomas, Kemba Walker, Chris Bosh, Andre Drummond, JJ Redick, DeMarcus Cousins, Wilt Chamberlain, Bradley Beal, Rudy Gobert, Aaron Gordon, Kristaps Porzingis, Nikola Vucevic, Andre Iguodala, Devin Booker, John Stockton, Jeremy Lin, Chris Paul, Pascal Siakam, Jayson Tatum, Gordon Hayward, Nikola Jokic, Bill Russell, Victor Oladipo, Luka Doncic, Ben Simmons, Shaquille O'Neal, Joel Embiid, Donovan Mitchell, Damian Lillard and *Giannis Antetokounmpo* in the Kindle Store. If you love football, check out my website at claytongeoffreys.com to join my exclusive list where I let you know about my latest books and give you lots of goodies.

Like what you read? Please leave a review!

I write because I love sharing the stories of influential athletes like Lamar Jackson with fantastic readers like you. My readers inspire me to write more so please do not hesitate to let me know what you thought by leaving a review! If you love books on life, sports, or productivity, check out my website at claytongeoffreys.com to join my exclusive list where I let you know about my latest books. Aside from being the first to hear about my latest releases, you can also download a free copy of *33 Life Lessons: Success Principles, Career Advice & Habits of Successful People*. See you there!

Clayton

References

"Lamar Jackson Stats." *Pro-Football Reference*. Nd. Web.

Dutton, Niel. "15 Crazy Stats from Lamar Jackson's Record-Breaking 2019 Season." *Ravens Wire*. 31 Dec 2019. Web.

"What Makes Lamar Jackson Special (Besides His Athleticism)? His Teammates Answer." *BaltimoreRavens.com*. 23 Nov 2019. Web.

[iv] Cadeaux, Ethan. "John Harbaugh and Lamar Jackson's Sideline Conversation is Caught on Tape." *NBC Sports*. 11 Nov 2019. Web.

[v] Willis, Zack. "Lamar Jackson's Life is More Tragic Than You Think." *SporsCasting.com*. 11 Jan 2020. Web.

[vi] "Lamar Jackson's Parents are the Inspiration for Ravens QB." *Heavy.com*. Nd. Web.

[vii] Walker, Childs. "How Lamar Jackson Used More Than Talent to Rise From the Fields of South Florida: 'He Continued to Work.'" *The Baltimore Sun*. 25 Nov 2019. Web.

[viii] Adelson, Andrea. "The Driving Force Behind Lamar Jackson's Success is his First Trainer – His Mom." *ESPN.com*. 1 Nov 2016. Web.

[ix] Leto, Matthew. "What if Lamar Jackson Stayed?" *ShSTheTribe.com*. 21 Nov 2016. Web.

[x] Jones, Jonathan. "Lamar Jackson, His Mother, and the Plan They've Always Had." *Sports Illustrated*. 3 Apr 2018. Web.

[xi] DePentima, Ryan. "Before NFL Dominance, Lamar Jackson's Star Shined Bright in Palm Beach County." *The Palm Beach Post*. 8 Jan 2020. Web.

[xii] Gonzalez, Hector. "Cook Runs Wild to Lead Miami Central Past Boynton Beach." *Miami Herald*. 16 Nov 2013. Web.

[xiii] Jones, Steve. "4-Star QB Commits to Louisville." *The Courier Journal*. 20 Aug 2014. Web.

[xiv] "Lamar Jackson College Stats." *Sports-Reference*. Nd. Web.

[xv] Johnson, Chris. "How Lamar Jackson Captivated the College Football World and Won the Heisman Trophy." *Sports Illustrated*. 10 Dec 2016.

[xvi] Chiusano, Anthony. "Top Five Heisman Moments from Lamar Jackson in 2016." *NCAA.com*. Nd. Web.

[xvii] Reid, Jason. "Lamar Jackson Gets a Chance to Prove Doubters Wrong. Ravens Must Also Do Their Part." *The Undefeated.* 27 Apr 2018.

[xviii] Lourim, Jake. "Lamar Jackson Caps a Successful Preseason with Ravens*." The Courier Journal.* 30 Aug 2018. Web.

[xix] Kasinitz, Aaron. "Baltimore Ravens Lamar Jackson Talks Up Joe Flacco: 'It's His Team Still.'" *PennLive.com. 12* Dec 2018. Web.

[xx] "Lamar Jackson Stats." *Pro-Football Reference.* Nd. Web.

[xxi] Cox, Dustin. "Baltimore Ravens Recap: Lamar Jackson Leads the Team to Victory in Debut." *BaltimoreBeatdown.com.* 18 Nov 2018. Web.

[xxii] McAtee, Riley. "Lamar Jackson's MVP Season Was Unlike Any Other." *TheRinger.com.* 1 Feb 2020. Web.

[xxiii] "'Not Bad for a Running Back' and Nine Other Classic Lamar Jackson Quotes from 2019." *NBC Sports.* 20 May 2020. Web.

[xxiv] Johnson, Martenzie. "Playoff Loss Doesn't Negate Lamar Jackson's Game-Changing Season." *The Undefeated.* 12 Jan 2020. Web.

[xxv] "Lamar Jackson Quotes." *Brainy Quote. Nd. Web.*

[xxvi] Miller, Hallie. "You've Heard About Lamar Jackson, the Star Ravens QB. Here's What We Know About Lamar Jackson the Person." *The Baltimore Sun.* 1 Dec 2019. Web.

[xxvii] "Who Is Lamar Jackson's Girlfriend? His Love Life in Detail." *Celeb Suburb.* 3 Sep 2020. Web.

[xxviii] "Lamar Jackson: Net Worth, Salary & Endorsements." *EssentiallySports.com.* Nd. Web.

[xxix] Chandler, Chris. "Lamar Jackson's $25,000 Donation Provides Meals to Students." *WLKY.com.* 26 Jan 2018. Web.

[xxx] Paylor, Terez. "Lamar Jackson's Dreams, Both On and Off the Field, Are as Alive as Ever." Yahoo Sports. 1 Oct 2020. Web.

[xxxi] Tinsley, Justin. "Baltimore Rookie Lamar Jackson is Into 21 Savage and NBA Young Boy – and Old School Miami Hurricanes Football." *The Undefeated.* 25 May 2018. Web.

[xxxi] "Kyler Murray Stats." *Pro-Football Reference.* Nd. Web.

[xxxiii] "17 Records, Feats, Benchmarks Lamar Jackson and the Ravens Hit on MNF." *BaltimoreRavens.com.* 26 Nov 2019. Web.

[xxxiv] "All the Impressive NFL Records Lamar Jackson Set Before His 23rd Birthday." *NBC Sports.* 7 Jan 2020. Web.

xxxv O'Connor, Ian. "Why John Harbaugh and Lamar Jackson Needed Each Other, and How Football Needed Them Together." *ESPN.* 20 Nov 2019. Web.

Made in the USA
Las Vegas, NV
24 October 2023

79656174R00069